THE GAL GUIDE

CHEATERS AND LIARS

HOW TO KNOW IF HE'S HAVING AN AFFAIR

THE GAL GUIDE

CHEATERS AND LIARS

HOW TO KNOW IF HE'S HAVING AN AFFAIR

THE EX-WHISPERER

First published by Level Best Books 2021

Copyright © 2021 by Gabrielle St. George

All rights reserved. No part of this publication may be reproduced, stored or transmitted in any form or by any means, electronic, mechanical, photocopying, recording, scanning, or otherwise without written permission from the publisher. It is illegal to copy this book, post it to a website, or distribute it by any other means without permission.

Gabrielle St. George asserts the moral right to be identified as the author of this work.

Author Photo Credit: Hooman Mesri Photography

First edition

ISBN: 978-1-68512-030-6

Cover art by Level Best Designs

This book was professionally typeset on Reedsy. Find out more at reedsy.com

This book is dedicated to all the great girlfriends out there, without whom we'd barely make it through the end of the week, never mind the end of the affair. Always ready to put the kettle on, or pour the wine and lend a sympathetic ear, a soft shoulder, tough love, and unfailing wisdom in our times of need. We owe our sanity to our BFFs. Thank you, gal pal.

Contents

Preface	iv
Praise for The Gal Guides	v
Chapter One	1
HAS A MAJOR CRIME BEEN COMMITTED?	1
(OR WERE YOUR FEELINGS ONLY ASSAULTED?)	1
WHAT DEFINITION OF MONOGAMY DID YOU AND YOUR PARTNER AGREE TO?	2
THE USUAL SUSPECTS	3
SUSPICIOUS BEHAVIOUR	4
MEANS, MOTIVE, AND OPPORTUNITY	6
HOW DO POLICE ESTABLISH MEANS, MOTIVE, AND OPPORTUNITY?	7
IS YOUR EVIDENCE CIRCUMSTANTIAL?	8
ARE YOU BEING RATIONAL OR ARE YOU F***ING FREAKING OUT?	10
Chapter Two	11
DO YOU HAVE PROBABLE CAUSE TO SUSPECT CHEATING?	11
(OR ARE YOU JUST INSECURE, JEALOUS, DRAMATIC, PARANOID?)	11
TRUST YOUR GUT INSTINCT	11
YOUR INTUITION IS YOUR ALLY	11
IGNORE YOUR BUILT-IN BULLSHIT DETECTOR AT YOUR PERIL	16

    A GOOD DETECTIVE ALWAYS TRUSTS
    THEIR GUT INSTINCT   16
    ARE YOU A CREDIBLE WITNESS?   17
    HOW CAN YOU BE SURE YOU'RE TUNED
    INTO YOUR INTUITION, AND NOT BEING
    TRICKED BY PARANOIA?   17
    TOP 3 SIGNS YOUR INTUITION IS SOUND-
    ING ALARM BELLS   20
Chapter Three   23
    HOW TO KNOW IF YOU HAVE ENOUGH EVI-
    DENCE TO CONVICT   23
        12 TELLTALE SIGNS HE'S HAVING AN AFFAIR   23
        THE NON-MYSTERIOUS NO-BRAINER
        SIGNS THAT HE'S CHEATING   38
Chapter Four   40
    HOW TO KNOW WHEN THE ACCUSED IS
    LYING THROUGH HIS TEETH   40
        GO UNDERCOVER TO CATCH HIM IN THE ACT   40
        THE LIE DETECTOR TEST   42
        HOW TO KNOW WHEN HIS PANTS ARE ON FIRE   42
        IT'S CALLED BODY "LANGUAGE" BECAUSE
        IT SPEAKS VOLUMES: 43
        BECOME FLUENT IN READING IT   43
        TOP 17 BODY LANGUAGE SIGNS THAT HE'S
        A BIG FAT LIAR   44
        BUILD UP YOUR BUILT-IN BULLSHIT DETECTOR: 47
        THE WAY HE SAYS THINGS REVEALS AS
        MUCH AS WHAT HE SAYS   47
        TOP 7 VERBAL SIGNS THAT HE'S PERJUR-
        ING HIMSELF   47
Chapter Five   50

HOW TO PROTECT YOUR RELATIONSHIP FROM A BREAK AND ENTER	50
IS YOUR RELATIONSHIP AT RISK OF A HOME INVASION?	50
14 DANGER SIGNS THAT YOUR RELATIONSHIP MAY BE DOA	51
6 WAYS TO BULLETPROOF YOUR RELATIONSHIP	52
DOES THE EVIDENCE SUPPORT THE CASE FOR THE UPSIDE OF AFFAIRS?	53
Conclusion	56
Acknowledgements	58
About the Author	59
Also by Gabrielle St. George	61

Preface

In order to protect the guilty I have changed the name of my cheating, lying, narcissistic, douche bag ex-husband to Lil Dick. Short Dick—I mean, Dick, for short. I know what you're thinking—She's bitter. I'm not bitter. I was bitter but now I'm better. In fact I'm better than better. I'm f***ing fantastic.

Dumping Dick was the best gift I ever gave myself. I paid a heavy price for my freedom, but it was worth every pound of flesh, every ounce of energy and every drop of dignity that I spent.

SPOILER ALERT— My reward for a long battle hard won in the trenches of divorce, was the life of my dreams. I got absolutely everything I deserved and unfortunately for Dick, so did he. Yes indeed, Karma bites.

Praise for The Gal Guides

"I'm pretty sure she wrote that book just for me! What a great book! The book is a quick read with everything you need to set yourself free from the relationship that has expired. I swear she has been following me around the last 3 years… it was spot on with my life. Thanks for the reassurance, I know I can do this FINALLY!" – Renee Bills, Goodreads Reviewer

"Really amusing and funny! I think her advice can be very useful for people who are struggling in their relationships. I'd definitely recommend it to someone who is having a hard time because it will help them see things from a different perspective—and laugh out loud along the way!" – Carmen Jimenez, Reviewer at The Girl From 61

"Absolutely loved the book, it's a cracker of a read, gets to the nitty gritty of finding out whether your boyfriend/girlfriend is a cheater and a liar… It's one of those books you can sit and read but with a fact finding practical guide at the same time… HIGHLY RECOMMENDED A MUST READ BOOK." – Pam Thomas, NetGalley Reviewer

Chapter One

HAS A MAJOR CRIME BEEN COMMITTED?

(OR WERE YOUR FEELINGS ONLY ASSAULTED?)

For thousands of years, people have married because their religion, culture, or laws have compelled them to do so. Today most of us get married because we want to, not because we have to. We get married because we desire commitment. Publicly most of us disapprove of infidelity, as witnessed by the constant falling from grace of our adored celebrities, sports stars, politicians, and religious heads, but privately more than half of us, are engaging in it ourselves. Virtually all recent research concurs that between 55% to 65% of people cheat on their partners.

Infidelity takes many forms: sexual, emotional, cyber (is it sex if you're not physically touching?), Whether or not your partner has been unfaithful to you entirely depends upon your definition of fidelity. For most of us, our understanding of monogamy is that we engage in sex and romance exclusively with our partner for the duration of our relationship. We allow these clearly drawn lines to be blurred when it comes to pornography, friendships, fantasizing about other people, and flirtations with work colleagues, neighbors, etc. The social, moral, and legal influences that have informed our definitions of monogamy in the past have evolved, whether or not we all like it.

Modern couples are acutely aware that a full half of the marriages out there will most definitely end in divorce and they proactively take steps to protect their relationships by expanding their definition of monogamy and negotiating a reality that suits them both. Commitment is not the same thing as monogamy. True commitment in a relationship is built on trust and honesty. An affair doesn't necessarily have to threaten a primary relationship if a couple has agreed to allow outside sexual liaisons, so long as the parties are open and honest with each other about these dalliances. For these couples, the destructive forces lay in the secret betrayals, the deceptions, the lying, and the hiding. Time will tell whether or not this new definition of monogamy will result in longer-lasting or happier relationships than their traditional forerunners.

WHAT DEFINITION OF MONOGAMY DID YOU AND YOUR PARTNER AGREE TO?

This can be consciously stated, or unconsciously felt, but it exists in every committed relationship. You both know what your spoken/unspoken relationship rules are and you both know when those rules have been broken. Maybe you and your partner have defined infidelity as having intercourse with someone else or engaging in certain sexual acts with another person. Maybe you have defined infidelity as being emotionally involved with someone else, as in sharing secrets and intimate feelings with that other person, or as just simply flirting.

These rules can be and perhaps should be renegotiated at different stages throughout the marriage. Our needs, desires, and understanding change with age, life stage, health, etc. We grow. We're not even the same people we were yesterday. It's realistic to expect that we could be spending 40 to 60 years with our life partner if we can stick it out for the long haul. As humans are we capable of remaining monogamous and sustaining love and romance with one person over such a long haul? Maybe, maybe not. One thing's for sure, the key to a healthy marriage is not clinging to outmoded rules that no longer serve us as a couple, or as individuals. The key to a healthy, happy relationship is open, honest communication with a good dose of realistic expectations and a deep level of understanding. This should be based in the reality that nothing ever stays the same and the knowledge that change is good and inevitable whether we want it or not. A committed relationship is a work in progress that requires both parties to come to the table regularly, with open minds and true hearts, to speak their piece.

So has a crime been committed? Has your partner betrayed you? That depends on your definition of monogamy. The definition you both agreed on. No one needs to tell you the answer to that. You know it and he knows it. If he has broken the rules that the two of you established in your relationship, then that is infidelity and he is guilty of harming your heart and that is no misdemeanor.

THE USUAL SUSPECTS

Every relationship is at risk of the occurrence of an affair and every one of us is capable of cheating, whether or not we wish to admit this fact. At the very least all of us have thought about cheating. Some of us full out fantasize about other people during sex with our present partner. We may fantasize about celebrities, work colleagues, or neighbors or flirt with friends and strangers. Some of us engage in cyber-flirting, posting a few too many likes on a certain someone's Facebook page, or anonymously cyberstalking a secret crush on Instagram.

Is this behavior cheating? Like I said earlier, it depends on how you define infidelity. Is it threatening to a relationship? The slippery slope potential is always there. But if everyone does it, doesn't that make it normal? I've never found a definition of "normal" that made sense to me, so let's not bother trying to figure that one out. The fact that everyone does it makes it just that, a fact—something true and real. Something we need to accept and be prepared to deal with. The Internet has facilitated infidelity for both sexes, all ages, all walks of life. A housewife stuck at home with no wheels, or cash, now has as much opportunity to cheat as my husband Dick did on his frequent, all expenses paid, weeks-long business trips to the South of France. Virtually everyone has the means and opportunity to screw around on their partner now. Does that make it normal? It makes it common. Does that make it acceptable? You be the judge (but only for your own relationship).

The fact is infidelity could happen anytime, anywhere, to anyone. No one is immune so don't kid yourself, but that doesn't mean it's a given in every single relationship, it's absolutely not. The potential for infidelity exists, but the potential to prevent it also exists. Being forewarned is forearmed.

SUSPICIOUS BEHAVIOUR

Perhaps you've had a nagging little feeling in the pit of your stomach that something is off in your relationship. Maybe you're even sensing that your partner has been unfaithful. You'll probably allow yourself to suffer this insecurity, breeding instability for some time until you can't handle not knowing the truth any longer. But how can you know for sure if your imagination is playing tricks on you or if your suspicions are justified? You have to follow your nose.

Initially, you may delicately ask your partner veiled questions and likely receive vague answers in response. These exchanges will not provide you with the information you are seeking and the chance of them allaying your fears are slim. Next, you'll feel you need to ramp things up in order to obtain the reassurance you're searching for. At this point, you may don protective body armor (just in case your suspicions turn out to be correct) and fully open the lines of communication with your partner by straight up asking him if he has cheated. It's possible that he'll tell you the truth, but unlikely. If he came clean about his affair or alternatively, if he professed his innocence and you had believed him, you would not be reading this book right now. Instead, he'll probably tell you that you're silly, crazy even, that you've always been a little insecure, or paranoid. He'll reassure you by telling you how beautiful you are and professing his undying love for you (establishing that he has no MOTIVE). He'll tell you that he could never lie to you, that he isn't capable of hurting you (establishing that he has no MEANS) and that you have nothing to worry about. How would he even find the time, or the energy to cheat on you (establishing that he has no OPPORTUNITY) what with his busy schedule and all?

Shortly after all this reassuring has settled in and later worn off, you'll find yourself back in the same place where you have languished ever since your first relationship insecurities arose. At this point, it's all on you to dig yourself out of that relationship shithole. It's time to take control of the situation, conduct your own investigation, establish guilt, or innocence and close the books on this case once and for all. Let's discuss how to go about that.

MEANS, MOTIVE, AND OPPORTUNITY

Police Investigation Techniques 101: MMO or Means, Motive, and Opportunity must be established to prove the accused guilty. A detective attempts to establish MMO at the very beginning of an investigation. You need to do this too. The vast majority of cases are solved simply and the guilty parties are usually the most obvious of the potential suspects. When a woman is assaulted or murdered the police always investigate her husband or boyfriend first because the simplest conclusion is most often the correct one in police investigations. Complex cases are rare, which is why Hollywood makes movies about them. Although advances in forensic science have changed the way evidence is collected and applied in investigations, most crimes are still solved the old-fashioned, boots to the pavement, way of knocking on doors, talking to people, and listening closely. Are you actually listening to what you're hearing? Listening and hearing are not the same things. Are you listening to what your partner is telling you? Are you listening to what your gut is telling you?

MEANS:
The ability of the defendant to commit the crime.
Ask yourself: Is he mentally and physically capable of cheating? In other words: Does he have a brain and a penis?

MOTIVE:
The reason the defendant committed the crime.
Ask yourself: Does he have a compelling reason to cheat? In other words, is he bored, sexually unsatisfied, neglected, or misunderstood at home? Is he deceitful, self-serving, or just an asshole?

OPPORTUNITY:

Whether the defendant had the chance to commit the crime (most often disproved by an alibi).

Ask yourself: Has he ever been out of your sight for more than 10 minutes? For a night? For a weekend? Travelled on a business trip? A fishing trip? Does he have private access to his own email and cell phone, which are not monitored 24/7 by you? In other words, is he more than 2 years old and are you his partner, not his mother?

HOW DO POLICE ESTABLISH MEANS, MOTIVE, AND OPPORTUNITY?

You've conducted your initial evaluation and now it's time to develop your case. You need to start collecting evidence. Obviously, individuals don't have access to much of the records that police do, but you'd be surprised what you can get your hands on with a little ingenuity. You're not going to be presenting your evidence in a court of law, so luckily for you, you don't need a search warrant to obtain it. You're the detective and you're the victim, but you're also the judge and jury in this case. You're the only one who needs to be convinced, beyond a reasonable doubt, that a crime has been committed. It might be helpful to your investigation for you to obtain some of the evidence through avenues the police routinely utilize such as:

- Interviews
- Witness Statements
- Inconsistent statements or lies
- Emails
- Text messages
- Social media posts
- Bank records

- Credit card statements
- Vehicle GPS
- Gas receipts
- Phone bills
- Airline tickets
- Photos
- Hotel and restaurant receipts
- Debts
- Addictions (gambling, drugs, alcohol, prostitutes, pornography)

How do you go about obtaining this evidence? By any means available. There are no rules or limits except your personal ethics and moral codes and you may feel the need to suspend a few of those for the purposes of your investigation. I know I did. I wouldn't normally look through people's desk drawers, pants pockets, car trunks, and bank statements, but I did what I had to do at the time and I'm not ashamed to admit it. All's fair in love and war.

IS YOUR EVIDENCE CIRCUMSTANTIAL?

Means, motive, and opportunity are all examples of circumstantial evidence, meaning they're not enough on their own to convict a person of a crime. The problem is that sometimes it's the only evidence available, so it's all we've got to work with.

People are convicted of crimes based on circumstantial evidence, but the evidence must be viewed as a whole, not as parts. A judge or jury must be convinced beyond a reasonable doubt that the only rational conclusion, based on all of the circumstantial evidence combined, is one of guilt and that there cannot be any other rational conclusion. A ruling of guilt cannot be based on speculation, it must be based on

CHAPTER ONE

reasoning through probability. Logic and common sense have to be applied to the evidence. The possibility of coincidence needs to be eliminated by considering the probabilities and improbabilities of the circumstantial evidence. Look closely at the facts before you. Is it possible that what you are seeing are mere coincidences? Are these possible coincidences so numerous that it seems unlikely that these amounts of random events would occur around one person or in one place or time? Are the circumstances surrounding the evidence so farfetched that believing them proves difficult?

In order to rule out the possibility of coincidence, you must calmly weigh the evidence. You can't do that if you have discovered fresh evidence and you are in a state of shock or you're feeling angry or out of control in any way. Having intense, emotionally charged reactions to bad news is to be expected, but before you pass any judgments, take a few steps back. You need to wait until you have collected yourself and you are in a mental state where you can approach the evidence rationally before you decide if your circumstantial evidence is worthy of a conviction. Make sure you have applied all of these parameters to the evidence that you have gathered in the case against your partner and then when you are ready, throw your emotion in the lockup. Logic is your best lead at the moment.

ARE YOU BEING RATIONAL OR ARE YOU F***ING FREAKING OUT?

You need to ask yourself the questions in the checklist below and be able to answer yes to all 5 of them before moving forward.

FREAK OUT CHECKLIST:

1. Are you able to focus on the big picture painted by the evidence as a whole, rather than fixating on separate bits of evidence?
2. When you look at all of the evidence combined is it clear that the only rational conclusion is one of guilt?
3. Have you ruled out the possibility that the evidence is merely a series of coincidences?
4. Are you applying logic and common sense to the evidence before you, rather than speculating?
5. Are you able to feel calm, grounded, and centered when you consider the evidence, or is it still crazy-making for you?

If you have answered yes to the 5 questions above then congratulations, you are being rational. A warning before you carry your investigation any further—make sure that you really do want to find out and can handle the truth. At some point, there will be no turning back. There aren't enough margaritas in the world to unsee a cheater cheating.

Chapter Two

DO YOU HAVE PROBABLE CAUSE TO SUSPECT CHEATING?

(OR ARE YOU JUST INSECURE, JEALOUS, DRAMATIC, PARANOID?)

TRUST YOUR GUT INSTINCT

YOUR INTUITION IS YOUR ALLY

Your intuition is like that wise old friend whose advice sounds kind of nutty in the moment, but who always winds up being able to say "I told you so" as she pours you another cup of comfort tea.

When I look back on the things in my life that I regret, big and small, I can see that they all have one thing in common. They are all the result of decisions I made despite my instincts telling me to make a different decision. I failed to listen to my heart and instead in those instances, I followed my head into the murky waters of overanalyzing. There the mind is often in a state of near-drowning from the exhaustion of obsessing over pros and cons and seeming facts and dearest wishes, which contradictions muddy the decision-making process. Many choices in life need to be made from a place of logical, rational thought, rather than from the intuitive, feeling place of the heart, but I have found this not to be the case when it comes to the most important ones. In these situations, the mind is the dark alley where regret lurks, waiting to mug your dreams, steal your joy and leave you nursing a lifelong wound of disappointment and remorse. When it comes to these major life choices, your heart is your safe house, your intuition your lighthouse.

I have often found that when we finally do make major, final decisions after long periods of deliberation, it is not only an all-encompassing feeling of relief that washes over us, it is also usually accompanied by an overwhelming knowing that we should have done this thing much, much earlier. We ask ourselves the question, why did we wait so long? Often we beat ourselves up for delaying what we now know was inevitable. We can be deluged with sadness and remorse for time lost. Try not to do this. It's pointless and it only results in you wasting even more time by dwelling in the past and wallowing in your weaknesses. Once you've made that life-changing choice, celebrate, dive in and swim with the current as swiftly as you can manage.

A month before I left my husband, a girlfriend gave me the phone number for an abuse hotline and urged me to call. At first, I thought she must have been joking. How dramatic, how inappropriate, how offensive. She persisted and persuaded me to call just to hear what a counselor might have to say.

It took a few days before I managed to dial the number and I felt like I was being melodramatic, disloyal even, by calling. When an abuse counselor answered the phone, I first apologized in advance for wasting her valuable time and told her that I was definitely not an abused woman and that I just had a question, but I didn't really have to ask it and I

CHAPTER TWO

could hang up and clear the line for any woman who might actually be in need of her essential services. The counselor did not want me to hang up. She had a soft and gentle voice that sounded patient and calm and knowledgeable. She sounded like someone who had received many calls that had started out exactly like mine with disclaimers and apologies. Abused women get used to saying sorry often. We spoke for an hour that day. The abuse counselor told me that the biggest mistakes she saw women make were when they failed to listen to that little voice inside them. She said that voice never lied and that it never steered you wrong. She told me that it was imperative for a person to trust their intuition and that ignoring it could be dangerous and even deadly in some cases.

I prefaced my question to the counselor by explaining how I was probably just being silly and paranoid and overreacting. I mean it's not against the law for a husband to be suspicious, or jealous, or controlling. The question I asked the abuse counselor was whether or not it was possible for my husband to stalk me.

Stalkers are usually deranged strangers or jilted ex-boyfriends. I didn't know if technically a husband could actually stalk his wife. When a husband acted like a stalker, was he just considered being a man "checking up on a spouse" even if done in an extreme fashion? Even if his behavior was causing his wife to feel hunted and frightened? Did a husband have the right to know where his wife was and what she was doing at all times? Even if she wasn't doing anything wrong? The counselor said that a woman's husband or boyfriend could absolutely be her stalker.

I persisted in telling the counselor that I was probably blowing little things out of proportion. I told her that I found out that my husband Dick had been checking my cell phone bills and recording notes on who had answered when he had re-dialed all the called numbers listed on my bill. I told her about the "List of Sins Committed" that I had found, where Dick had written down every slight he felt I had ever inflicted on him over the years. These so-called sins of mine including going to my best girlfriend's home for a cocktail one evening and taking my children on a vacation with my sister, her children, and our mother, which my mother paid for (it was an Alaskan cruise and Dick suffered from seasickness). I told the counselor that my eldest son had been sleeping in my bed for the past two months because he felt scared for me when his father was home, as he was verbally and physically threatening. (My husband had moved into a spare bedroom in the basement by that time.) I told her that one dark night at three am my son and I watched out my bedroom window as my husband searched my vehicle with a flashlight and removed a small, black box from underneath the car, that looked like it might be a GPS or some sort of tracker. There were many more examples of similar, unusual, but I emphasized probably insignificant instances. I told the abuse counselor that I had a wild imagination so I knew I probably shouldn't trust myself and was likely reading far too much into these small, seemingly silly occurrences.

The abuse counselor disagreed. I was shocked when she responded by telling me that I wasn't crazy and that she believed I was in danger. This concept, this validation, was difficult for me to accept and I tried to brush it off with protests that perhaps I was being paranoid, that my fear was irrational. I thought she was overreacting. The counselor emphatically stated that my son was an 18-year-old man and he was also afraid for me, so that was a clear indicator that I wasn't being irrational in my fear of my husband. She advised me to take my children and go to a shelter immediately. She told me that in her professional opinion I wasn't safe and she urged me to seek help right away.

Later I felt relieved to have been told by an expert that I wasn't paranoid, or crazy. But there was a flipside that took a while to sink in. It took some time for me to wrap my head around the fact that my living situation wasn't normal, or acceptable, that my husband's behavior was a form of emotional abuse, and that I was a victim. How did I end up here? How did my once happy family life spiral into this place of suspicion and potential danger? Initially, this truth felt completely disabling, but as I swiftly made the decision to no longer accept this treatment, nor these circumstances as my normal, this knowledge immediately transformed my attitude to one of empowerment. There was only one option for me and that was to put an end to the unhealthiness and unhappiness of the situation for myself and for my children.

I didn't go to a shelter because I couldn't leave my pets behind, but I formulated a plan to protect myself and my children that was workable for me, and I figured out the details in order to implement it as soon as I possibly could. Dick was leaving on a weeklong business trip in two weeks' time. I would remain alert and tread carefully for the next fourteen days and as soon as he left for his trip, I would pack him up and put him out while he was away. I knew what I had to do and I had two weeks to do it.

My husband had made our home into a landmine-laden, tightrope act for me and our four children to navigate. I had underestimated how difficult it would be to walk on eggshells and ensure that I didn't rock any boats while keeping my plan a secret for fourteen very long days. Dick was more easily upset, getting angrier and watching me more closely with each passing day. I struggled to go about my daily business wearing a pasted-on facial expression that I hoped would pass as "normal" and wouldn't sound any alarm bells. If Dick had picked up the scent of anything that might've raised his suspicions that I could be up to something, he would have canceled his business trip and my entire plan would have gone up in smoke. I would have lost the one foreseeable chance I had to remove him from our home and I knew for certain that I'd never take another breath without him knowing when and where I did so.

Those two weeks were the longest ones of my life and his last night with us was one of his most volatile, but the children and I survived it. The next time my husband left our house was the last time he left our house.

IGNORE YOUR BUILT-IN BULLSHIT DETECTOR AT YOUR PERIL

A GOOD DETECTIVE ALWAYS TRUSTS THEIR GUT INSTINCT

You can too. And you should. That gnawing feeling in the pit of your stomach, that tiny voice in the back of your brain that refuses to shut up no matter how often you attempt to silence it, is there to help you. Let it. Trust it. It will never lie to you, never let you down. You were born with your keen sense of intuitiveness, but it's a muscle you need to exercise regularly in order for it to develop and grow as it should. Work your Spidey Senses by using them and respecting them. Your intuition is one of your greatest resources and your most reliable indicator for gauging what's right for you and what's not, what's real and what's fantasy, what's safe, and what's dangerous. It's a gift, appreciate it. Tune into it, but don't become paranoid. You know the difference. If you ever feel unsure, then get grounded first and tune into it again.

The hard truth is that if you really do suspect that your partner is cheating on you, then he probably is. I've never personally known anyone who truly suspected this and later came to find out that they were entirely wrong. Studies show that a full 85% of women who suspect that their partner is cheating on them turn out to be correct. That old saying, "The wife is always the last one to know", is often true, but not because the clues weren't there. There are almost always signs, some more obvious than others, but they are there to be found if one looks for them. Those partners who find out last are likely the ones who really did not want to know that their world had changed, that their relationship expectations, shared hopes and dreams of love had disintegrated, while they purposely looked the other way. The good news is that endings, no matter how difficult, always beget new beginnings. Your instincts will protect you if you allow them to. Trust them. Trust yourself.

ARE YOU A CREDIBLE WITNESS?

HOW CAN YOU BE SURE YOU'RE TUNED INTO YOUR INTUITION, AND NOT BEING TRICKED BY PARANOIA?

Off the top, I am ruling out the possibility that your issues may result from the reality that you are suffering from some deep psychological illness. If that is the case neither myself, nor any book can help you. You need to seek professional medical advice. I am speaking to the rest of us, who suffer from the common malady of the pain in the ass, human condition.

Paranoia is an extreme level of fear. We usually experience fear because of negative experiences we have had in our past. Perhaps you are afraid that your current partner is going to cheat on you because that's what your father did to your mother, or what your last partner did to you. Maybe the anxiety you're feeling is a result of all the emotional baggage you've carried with you into your current relationship. Fear is a highly charged emotion that can easily overtake all our other emotions, as well as our common sense and rational thought if we allow it to get out of control. Fear usually focuses on our worries about the future. Fear can interfere with our intuition. Do you actually have a legitimate reason to suspect that your partner is cheating on you? Or do you feel undeserving of having a partner who is trustworthy and do you expect that he will leave you? Are you projecting your personal issues and fears onto your partner? If this is the case you need to seek professional help to deal with your self-esteem issues before they destroy your relationship. Your relationship may be a very good one and if it is, then you most definitely do deserve to have it. If you don't have access to a therapist or counselor, then speak to a trusted friend, read books from the library, or at least go online and find reputable websites that can refer you to the resources (often free) that can help you.

Your intuition, your gut instincts, are extremely reliable. You can trust them and you need to listen to them. Instincts exist to provide us with basic survival skills. They are not thoughts that we hem and haw over. When it comes to a matter of survival, we do not make lists of pros and cons, we take action and our body tells us what to do, not our brain. Your body has its own, deep intelligence. Believe it when it attempts to communicate with you and provide you with answers that you can be assured, are always correct. Your intuition is not emotional, it is grounded and realistic. It occurs in the present moment, not in the past or future. Your intuition always reacts to and communicates in the here and now. Be here now and listen to it when it speaks to you.

When you are called upon to make major life decisions it is important to take the time you need to consider the pros and cons of the options presented to you. It's important to think things through and analyze the situation. What you don't want to do is become stuck in the muck and mire of overthinking things. That is when confusion gives way to disorientation in the decision-making process. That is when you get scared and end up making very poor choices because you make them from a place of fear, which is a place of powerlessness. You never want to be there. You want to make all your important decisions from a place of empowerment. That is where you make healthy choices that

CHAPTER TWO

positively impact your life.

As you make decisions in the course of your relationship, take your own temperature. How are you feeling? Are you feeling calm, centered, at peace? Good, you are on the right track then. Let's say you have made the decision to trust your partner, set aside your suspicions of him cheating, and set to work on increasing your self-esteem and your sense of deserving all good things in love and life. Moving forward, if you have feelings of calmness, centeredness, and peace, then you were right to trust your partner. Carry on.

However, if you have made this decision and you are doing the necessary work and that nagging feeling of distrust and doubt persists at churning your stomach upside down and that little voice in the back of your brain keeps emitting warning bells telling you that something smells rotten, then you need to re-evaluate your decision. These persistent, negative feelings in your body are a sign that you are not on the right track. Pay attention to them. Your mind may play tricks on you, but unless you are a hypochondriac, your body tells you the truth. It feels like something is off because something is off. It's not complicated. Don't look for excuses to deny the facts, or postpone the inevitable. Open your eyes, face the reality of your situation and take control of it. You can do this. You may not know if you're right, or wrong, but you do know that you need to know for sure, one way or the other. Time to grab this bull by the horns and find out what's real once and for all. Knowledge is power. Always.

TOP 3 SIGNS YOUR INTUITION IS SOUNDING ALARM BELLS

1. IT'S TELLING YOU YOU'RE IN PHYSICAL DANGER

Do not second-guess yourself when you get this strong feeling. Pay attention even if it's just a vague vibe of creepiness. If you're sensing that harm could be lurking nearby do not shrug off the warning and tell yourself that you're just being silly, or melodramatic (like I did). Likewise, if you get the feeling that something isn't right with your body don't wait too long before making a doctor's appointment. Our physical body has its own intelligence and is a great communicator. It's your job to listen and respond.

You know those scenes in horror flicks where all the warning signs are glaringly obvious that the killer is inside the darkened house and the next victim ventures into the basement, alone, with only a flashlight, anyway? They die and nearly annoy us viewers to death. Don't be that dumbass B Movie character. If your instincts tell you that a threatening someone, or something, is waiting around the next corner, in the parking lot, following you on the street, or for God's sakes lurking in your basement—Get out! Turn around and run to the nearest, building, crowd, or police station. You've been given a built-in alarm system for a reason, don't ignore it.

2. IT'S TELLING YOU THIS PERSON YOU JUST MET IS NOT WHAT THEY SEEM

I'm not referring to the full-on creeps we can all sniff out a mile away. We know those people straight off when we encounter them. It's those other, trickier ones we have to concern ourselves with. The charismatic ones. Those people who come across as great, friendly, personable, and are experts at making superb first impressions. But there is just something a little…off about them, something that doesn't quite ring true and authentic. This is usually a niggling, small feeling that's hard to put a finger on, and sometimes we feel guilty over our sense of wariness like maybe we're being judgey and unfair. The truth is, we usually come to find out that our instincts were correct. There was a reason our intuition told us to beware at worst, this wolf in sheep's clothing, and at best, false advertising of a book that wasn't anything like it's cover.

3. IT'S TELLING YOU YOU'RE ON THE WRONG PATH

We're lucky when we see flashing, neon signs and massive, milestone markers along our chosen paths to confirm for us that we're on the right road. It's always a comfort to know we are headed in the direction that we're meant to be going in. Sometimes the signs are subtle and the only way for us to know for sure that we are where we're supposed to be, doing what we're supposed to be doing, is the knowledge that things feel good, feel right, feel comfortable. Feeling good is an excellent indicator. When things feel crappy, stressful, confusing, or even just a little bit off or uncomfortable, then it is time to tune in and listen up to that little voice inside. It will be trying to communicate a message to you and has probably been attempting to do so for quite some time but has gone unheard. If you pay attention to your intuition in times like these, you will hear loud and clear that the path you are following is not the right one for you. When we do receive the message sometimes it's not what we want to hear. Perhaps we've invested a great deal of time, or energy, or money into this path that we bet on as the right one for ourselves and the thought of jumping ship is not an option we wish to consider. So, we hear the message, but we turn the volume down and carry on travelling along that wrong path anyway. This strategy never works. This only prolongs the agony of the inevitable. And if you're really stubborn the Universe is not averse to knocking you flat on your ass. Literally. I've known people who have had freak accidents that landed them in hospital, forcing them off a career or life path they had resolutely clung to despite the fact that the journey was making them completely miserable. And then there are those who have been shocked to witness their relationship implode in full-out nuclear meltdown mode because they refused to acknowledge a multitude of earlier warning signs that clearly demonstrated their union was in trouble. These naïve souls are left feeling completely blindsided when the destined and unavoidable breakdown in their love life finally did occur, despite their best efforts to ignore the obvious.

Whatever life path you're sailing along, it should feel like you're drifting downstream effortlessly, elegantly, going with the flow. If you're fighting against a bitch of a current, struggling to keep your head above choppy waters, I hate to break it to you, but you're pointed in the wrong direction. You're never going to get to where you want to be and this shit show of a journey is going to bring you more pain and anguish than you ever bargained for. Let go. Give in. Stop struggling. Flow downstream towards happy.

Chapter Three

HOW TO KNOW IF YOU HAVE ENOUGH EVIDENCE TO CONVICT

12 TELLTALE SIGNS HE'S HAVING AN AFFAIR

In a nutshell, it all comes down to changes in your partner's behavior. If he is suddenly looking, acting, sounding differently than he has in the past, then you may find your Spidey Senses aroused for good reason. If your partner is exhibiting only a couple of the following signs, it may not be prudent to jump to the conclusion that he is in fact cheating. However, if your SO is demonstrating a good number of these signs, then chances are you have a legitimate cause for concern. As the Wise Ones say, where there's smoke there's fire.

SIGN #1 MYSTERIOUS TELEPHONE HABITS

- He often receives weird calls. When you ask him who it was, he tells you they're wrong numbers or hang-ups. You may also be getting a lot of hang-ups if you answer his phone for him. Usually, with wrong numbers people will ask to speak to somebody before they realize they've misdialed, but after you say hello there's silence and

then a hang-up.
- He tries to answer the phone before you can get to it. He never ever leaves his cell phone lying around. In fact, it's usually on his body and he even takes it with him whenever he uses the bathroom. He does not allow you to use it.
- If you ever do get access to his phone you see text messages from friends, or colleagues whose names you don't recognize i.e., they're fake names.
- He often leaves the room to carry on his conversations in private and, even then uses a hushed voice.
- When you check the phone bill there is one number you don't recognize that is called a lot, at all hours.
- You walk into the room and he hangs up quickly, speaks quietly, or acts weirdly.
- He is talking or texting on his phone A LOT.
- He deletes the name and number info from his Caller ID list.
- He deletes his old text messages, sometimes as soon as he's finished sending or receiving them. Most people don't do this unless their phone memory is full which rarely happens.
- Same goes for deleting voice messages.
- You find out he has a cell phone you didn't know about. (Even worse if it's a separate account that is billed elsewhere, such as to his business.)

A friend of mine once received a call from a stranger who said he had found her cell phone in a parking lot outside a neighborhood sports bar and had dialed the number listed as "Home." The man wasn't far away and he offered to drop the phone off to her. She was at home cooking dinner for her young children so she gratefully accepted the kindness. The Good Samaritan dropped her husband's cell phone off a few minutes later. Her husband had guarded that cell phone like it

CHAPTER THREE

contained the codes to nuclear weapons of mass destruction. And in a way it did. What she found on it that evening blew her marriage up. She had enough time before her husband walked through the door to read hundreds of the most X-rated texts imaginable to and from numerous women, over long periods of time. Fate had intervened, forcing her to open her eyes and see.

SIGN #2 MYSTERIOUS COMPUTER HABITS

- You're not allowed to use his computer. Ever. He's got it protected with a password that you are not privy to.
- When he's on his computer and you walk into the room, he often closes it, or switches screens.
- He's on his computer A LOT, especially late at night.
- He stays up long after you go to bed to "work", or "game" on his computer.
- He has email and social media accounts that he's hidden from you.
- He erases his history regularly.
- He is constantly, obsessively checking his email.
- He starts deleting emails and emptying his email trash, almost as soon as he receives them.
- He doesn't share his passwords with you for any of his social media sites and doesn't like you to look at his Facebook or Instagram pages, or the chatrooms he visits.

A girlfriend of mine had a husband who had always been extremely secretive regarding his computer. His best friend lived in another country and was dying of cancer. My friend agreed that her husband should plan a holiday with his ill buddy before it was too late. The two men planned a week in Mexico and my girlfriend booked her husband's flight for him and drove him to the airport. When she arrived back home, she found that her husband had mistakenly left his email password out on his desk.

The temptation to open his email account was too great to resist and I doubt many people would have been able to. My friend opened Pandora's Box.

She found emails from her husband's supposedly terminally ill friend, who was in fact healthy as a horse, had no plans to travel anywhere but had agreed to serve as the cover story for his buddy's Mexican mayhem. She also read loads of raunchy messages from the woman her husband was actually rendezvousing with on the Mayan Riviera. The new couple was so excited to share their first holiday together.

How sweet.

Seven days later this cheater was surprised when my girlfriend wasn't waiting at the airport to pick him up like they had prearranged. He was even more surprised when he discovered that everything he owned had been packed into his car, and his vehicle parked in the lot at his girlfriend's apartment. My friend never let the lying cad cross the threshold of their family home again.

SIGN #3 MYSTERIOUS VEHICLE HABITS

- You find hairs, lipstick smudges, perfume scents, phone numbers, or heaven forbid, panties, or a condom that don't belong to you.
- You check the odometer on his vehicle (if you're doing this you're not trying to figure out if he's cheating, you're gathering evidence to make your case) and he's been doing a lot more driving than usual, or there is less mileage than there should be since he told you he had to drive out of town last weekend for a business conference.
- When errands that should take a few minutes last hours and he always has a ream of excuses for the delay, like inexplicably long lineups, running into an old friend who chatted endlessly, having

car trouble, or running out of gas.
- He suddenly keeps the car much cleaner than he used to and especially likes to remove the kid's toys and belongings from it.
- You get in the passenger seat and it has been readjusted from the position you always keep it in.
- He keeps things hidden in the trunk, like toiletries, or a change of clothes, or receipts and bills.

When I finally looked, late one night while my husband was taking a shower, I found a box of Dick's Visa and cell phone bills locked in the trunk of his vehicle. I went through them and found three phone numbers I didn't recognize that he called a lot, at all hours, including times when I knew him to be sitting on planes waiting for takeoff when he went on business trips. He even called these numbers long distance while he was away in other countries. I tracked the numbers and found that they belonged to a recently separated woman whom we knew slightly, whose children attended the same school as our children. One number was her cell, one was her workplace and the other was her home phone. The Visa bills revealed expensive dinners with bottles of wine at restaurants I had never been to, some on nights when my husband had returned hours late from business trips because, he told me, his plane had been delayed.

SIGN # 4 MYSTERIOUS NEW CLEANLINESS HABITS

- He smells different. It could be another woman's perfume, or unfamiliar soap, or shampoo because he's showering somewhere else.
- He smells the same as he did when he left for work—i.e., he showered before returning home.
- He jumps in the shower as soon as he arrives home and he's not in

the construction trade.
- He's wearing new cologne. And he's wearing a lot more of it than he ever did before.

When I finally snooped through my husband's bathroom cabinet, I found an array of grooming products that I had no idea he used, including a back waxing kit and a box of hair dye. There were also numerous receipts for a manicure and massage spa near his office where Dick seemed to spend many lunch hours. I hadn't noticed that he had particularly trimmed cuticles and buffed nails, so I had to wonder if he wasn't having another part of his anatomy rubbed and tugged.

SIGN # 5 MYSTERIOUS NEW PERSON WHO TAKES UP A LOT OF HIS TIME

- He starts spending way too much time with another person. This could be someone at work, a friend, or a neighbor.
- He's suddenly constantly volunteering to help out a friend with projects around their home, or with their work tasks.
- He spends time making preparations for special kindnesses or spends money on thoughtful gifts for this person. This level of niceness is out of character for him and you are not on the receiving end of his newly generous spirit.
- He talks about another woman, whom you have never met, a lot.
- He seems a little too enthusiastic about this new person and when you ask about her, he tells you that she is "just a friend."
- He relays bits of their conversations to you, repeating interesting things she's said that he is stoked over and he expresses new thoughts and opinions that seem to come out of left field.
- He may be thinking about this woman so much that it's next to impossible for him not to mention her. He also likes to say her

name out loud.
- He tells you tiny bits and pieces because it eases his guilt to make safe, quasi, mini confessions.

A few months before I put my husband out of our home, I returned from the morning run of driving the kids to school, to find Dick and a much younger woman standing in the middle of our kitchen. It seemed that he was showing her through the house. I was thrown by their presence, so I was polite when he introduced us, but probably not overly friendly. The woman was a new work colleague I had never met and she seemed extremely uncomfortable with the whole scenario. Dick explained that she was having her car serviced and he had volunteered to pick her up from the garage earlier that morning and drive her to their office. He said he had to return home to pick up something he had forgotten. Our home was very far out of their way so this didn't make any sense, but I knew what he was doing. Our house was a very grand and gorgeous new house on 100 beautiful acres. Dick was a show-off, a performer, and he was doing backflips to impress the young woman. I was pretty sure it wasn't working for him. In any event, my arrival definitely cramped his style and they departed quickly after my presence dropped the curtain on his show. He never did get to show her the bedrooms.

SIGN # 6 MYSTERIOUS NEW AVERSION TO SPENDING TIME WITH FAMILY, OLD FRIENDS, AND YOU

- He's too busy to attend family gatherings or social activities with friends.
- When he does attend, he shows up late, or leaves early. Carrying on an affair takes up an inordinate amount of time and energy.
- He'll likely blame a newly heavy workload for his time crunch, but he's probably spending that time with another person, even if only

online, or on the phone.
- He avoids attending social gatherings with you, probably because he doesn't want certain people to know you are still together and functioning as a regular couple.
- When you are together around friends or his work colleagues he acts uncomfortable around you and you get the strong sensation that everyone else is also uncomfortable. This is probably because they know he's cheating on you, but could also be the result of all the horrible stories he's told them about you to justify his cheating to himself.
- He spends a lot more time on his own and a lot less time with you.
- He excludes you from most of his activities, including work functions.
- He may have taken up a new sport or hobby to which he devotes a great deal of time.

Shortly before our separation my husband, a workaholic who left for work by 7 am and never got home before 9 each night, suddenly found the time to join a co-ed Badminton league and had started taking yoga classes at a local studio for the first time in his life. I would have loved to have done yoga myself, but as a virtual single mom when it came to running four kids around five nights a week and Saturdays to karate, ballet, swimming, football, soccer, music lessons, theatre, tutoring, part-time jobs, helping with their homework and feeding them, extracurriculars for myself weren't on the radar and wouldn't be for a number of years to come.

Dick skipped out on our last couple of family Easter dinners because he said he was swamped with work on his income tax returns, even though he was years behind in filing them anyway. The writing was on the wall, but I guess I was too busy raising four kids to take notice. The Universe had to hit me over the head with a sledgehammer before

I finally opened my eyes and saw. And boy, did I ever get a hell of a whack on the noggin when that day finally came.

SIGN # 7 MYSTERIOUS CHANGE IN HIS ATTITUDE TOWARD YOU

- He is often irritable and easily angered.
- He is extremely critical of you and often sarcastic. It's easier for him to cheat on you if he focuses on the things he doesn't like about you and it makes him feel his cheating is justified.
- He is generally unhappy and dissatisfied most of the time without providing any explanation for his feelings.
- He is more controlling and involved in everything you are doing.
- He asks a lot of questions about your schedule wanting to know where you will be at most times. (This is not because he is interested in you and what you're doing. He does this to minimize the chances of him getting caught doing what he's doing).
- He is uninterested and disconnected from you and your relationship.
- He does not respond to your attempts at being affectionate. For most of us, it's difficult to love or be invested in two people at the same time. He's choosing to focus on her.
- He berates you for being affectionate especially for any PDAs. (You never know who might see and report back to his girlfriend).
- He is more self-involved and oblivious to everyone and everything else around him.
- He accuses you of cheating. He may feel guilty, be projecting, or be attempting to deflect thoughts you may be having about what he's up to. If he's cheating and has realized how easy it is to do, he may wonder if you're doing it too.
- He may pick fights to create an excuse to sleep on the couch, or

storm out of the house (so he can go see, or talk to her). If he doesn't have to speak to you for a while, he doesn't have to lie to you for a while and that makes his life easier.
- He stops talking to you. There is no such thing as long, heartfelt conversations anymore, as he manages to turn discussions into blowups almost immediately. He's afraid you'll see through him if you look at him too closely. He may even avoid looking you in the eye for the same reason.
- He needs space and is suddenly emotionally distant, accusing you of breathing down his neck, or of distrusting him. He has put up walls that protect him from the danger of you getting close enough to read him.
- He is much happier than he has been in ages. (Affairs can have that effect).
- He helps out around the house more, virtually whistling while he works. (He's thinking lots of "happy thoughts"—not about you).
- He buys you more gifts and gives you more compliments than he used to. (To relieve his guilt—he's got a lot to hide).
- He is more enthusiastic, energetic, and more loving and attentive. (In an exaggerated attempt to throw you off any scent that his true affections lay elsewhere).

A girlfriend of mine went through her husband's sock drawer and found a velvet jewelry box that contained a diamond belly button ring. The receipt was with it. It was extremely expensive and with three little girls, they were strapped for cash. It was also purchased from a jewelry store on the other side of the country where he had taken a recent business trip, so he couldn't return the bauble. My girlfriend's only body piercings were in her ears. She confronted her husband and he claimed that he bought it hoping that one day she might decide to get her belly button pierced and then he planned to give it to her. When a cheater is caught off guard his excuses made on the fly are usually pathetically unconvincing. Shortly afterward the diamond stud disappeared from his drawer.

SIGN #8 MYSTERIOUSLY LONG WORK HOURS

- He is suddenly putting in a lot more hours at work.
- These extra hours worked are not reflected in his paychecks.
- He doesn't invite you to work functions, or any get-togethers with his colleagues.
- He is frequently unavailable when you call him at work, doesn't return your calls until hours later, or asks you not to call him at work at all.
- His cell phone is turned off for hours at a time and he tells you he didn't have any cell service during those periods.
- He has business meetings that last late into the night, or all night long.
- He has weekend-long conferences that are so time-consuming he tells you that he can't call you and you shouldn't bother trying to reach him.
- The frequency, or the length of his business trips increases.
- His work-related expenses increase so that he is bringing less money home.
- He constantly comes home late from work.
- He constantly complains about how stressful his work is, blames that stress on his new behavior, and does not want to discuss it any further.

SIGN #9 MYSTERIOUS CHANGE IN THE WAY HE ACTS AROUND THE HOUSE

- He rushes to pick up the mail and secrets away his credit card bills and cell phone bills before you can see them.
- He loses interest in doing chores around the house that he used to do religiously, like mowing the lawn, taking out the garbage, fixing leaky faucets.
- He's far less invested in the children and has little patience with them.
- He loses interest in the kids entirely. He's often too busy to spend time with them and when he does, he's distracted and forgetful. The one thing he does volunteer for is driving the children to their extra-curricular activities. These get him out of the house and free him up to make and receive phone calls.
- He has a newfound interest in doing laundry. (He's got some incriminating evidence to clean up).
- He's listening to different kinds of music, watching new sorts of movies and TV shows that "a friend" has recommended to him.
- He's tired all the time and takes lots of long naps. (A chance to indulge his happy daydreams).
- He no longer goes to bed at the same time as you.

There was a period of about a year, late in my marriage where my husband, who never slept much, announced every Friday night, after getting home from work late, that he felt restless and needed to get out of the house. This would occur after the children were sleeping and I had gotten into bed and was nearly asleep, if not zonked right out from a long, hectic week of chauffeuring four busy kids around, running a large house, and doing my own work. We're talking 11 pm or so. Dick would ask half-heartedly if I wanted to drag my exhausted body out of bed, get dressed, and go for a drive with him. Even on a frigid winter's night. Jokes? He knew I wouldn't voluntarily rouse myself from my warm bed to go driving in the dark along empty streets.

CHAPTER THREE

Who would? We lived in a small town. Nothing would be open other than the 24-hour coffee shop where he said he would pick up a tea at the drive-thru and proceed to cruise around, basically in circles. He would probably have been the only car on the road most nights.

After months of this Friday night ritual of his, I finally took him up on his offer to join him and he seemed genuinely annoyed. I climbed out of bed and threw a coat over my pajamas. We got a tea at the drive-thru and proceeded to wind aimlessly through the dark, suburban streets of the sleeping, boring town. Dick didn't seem to be enjoying himself.

I realize now that I probably interfered with a rendezvous, or delayed an awaited phone conversation. After an hour I suggested we go home. Dick dropped me off and went back out for another couple of hours.

One Friday night he didn't go out driving. He never went out driving around alone in the dark again. Break up?

SIGN #10 MYSTERIOUS CHANGES IN HIS APPEARANCE

- He's bought himself a new wardrobe, even though he's always professed to hate shopping and up until now has worn whatever you've purchased for him and hung in his closet.
- His new wardrobe is decidedly different from his usual style of dressing.
- He's got a new hairstyle, has either grown a beard or shaved his beard off. (Not because you have been asking him to do this forever).
- He's discovered men's moisturizers and hair sculpting gel.
- He's dying his hair, waxing his back, going for manicures, wearing a new cologne, had his teeth whitened, or finally had those unsightly moles removed.
- He's grooming down there.
- He's changed his diet and is losing weight. Your meat and potatoes mainstay man has a newfound interest in keto or veganism.

- He's off the couch with no prodding from you and is hitting the gym regularly.
- He is newly meticulous about his grooming habits.
- He's finally thrown out all his ripped, stained, and holey boxers, purchased new briefs, and no longer wears mismatched socks.
- He dresses up more for work.
- He dresses up more for every occasion.
- His eyes are brighter, twinkling with excitement the way they used to around you a long time ago.
- His complexion has a healthy glow, or ruddiness, like the kind you get after having robust sex.

SIGN #11 MYSTERIOUS CHANGES IN BED

- His sex drive suddenly plummets.
- When you initiate sex, he turns you down. (Unless he's joined a monastery, he's getting his sexual needs met elsewhere).
- He no longer wants to kiss you.
- His sex drive suddenly increases. An exciting new partner and greater frequency of sex raises testosterone levels, which he may bring home to the bed he shares with you.
- He has a newfound interest in porn.
- He has a newfound interest in experimenting sexually. This could include kink that the two of you have never discussed, or engaged in before but he has been recently introduced to.
- He performs new tricks in bed. (He had to have learned them from somewhere).
- He has scratches, bruises, or bite marks on his back, or chest, or (do I actually have to state this one?) hickeys on his neck.

CHAPTER THREE

At some point in our marriage, my husband began complaining that I never initiated sex. This may have been during the period where, having given birth to four children in five years, in the service of their care, I proceeded to run around like a chicken with my head cut off, twenty-four hours a day, for a decade and a half. Once when my family holidayed in Disney World with my sister, her husband, and kids, we all spent an evening in the concierge lounge of our hotel, the four adults imbibing in the complimentary champagne and canapés, while the children happily played games around us. I especially enjoyed the champagne—overly enjoyed it shall we say. When we went to our rooms, I tipsily got the kids settled on the beds in one of our adjoining suites with snacks and a Disney movie. When my husband Dick emerged from the shower, I locked the door between the rooms and proceeded to address his lack of initiation complaint about me. He was stoked. He was all in. He was satiated and smiling ear-to-ear well before the kids started knocking on the closed door (which wasn't too long later but long enough). But just before I returned to attend to the children, Dick grabbed me by the arm and spat venom, "You're drunk. You would have fucked any man who had of been in this room." And that my friends, may hold a clue as to why I might have been reluctant to initiate sex with my husband.

SIGN #12 MYSTERIOUS LEVEL OF DEFENSIVENESS

- He becomes extremely defensive when you question him about where he has been, why he is so late, or what he has been doing and with whom.
- He is generally more secretive about everything he does.
- He always suggests that you call his same friend, or work colleague, who will verify where he has been. He knows you won't call this person.

- He is always too exhausted to talk when he does arrive home.
- He is constantly saying how stressed out he is, which is how you know he will lose it and there will be a fight if you persist in questioning him, so you don't.
- He is guilt-ridden, which makes him generally bad-tempered.

My husband would pick fights out of the blue and when he would end them by storming out of our bedroom with his pillow in his arms like a category-5 cyclone, I would be left sitting on the edge of the bed dumbfounded, not knowing what I could have possibly done to provoke this nuclear fission. Dick would then spend months sleeping in our son's bed. Do you think these may have been the time periods he was involved with somebody else? It never occurred to me then. Head in the sand syndrome, I suppose.

THE NON-MYSTERIOUS NO-BRAINER SIGNS THAT HE'S CHEATING

- He stops wearing his wedding band.
- He has lipstick on his collar.
- He has female hairs on his clothes that do not belong to you or your golden retriever.
- He is acting erratically.
- He gets a mysterious phone call and leaves the house without any explanation.
- He is newly, overly enthusiastic in encouraging you to go out with the girls or to go away on solo trips.
- When you catch him in lies.
- When he forgets plans he made with you.
- When he forgets your birthday or anniversary.

CHAPTER THREE

- When he starts flirting with women, or with a specific woman, while he is with you.
- When he guards his cell phone with his life.
- When he comes home in the middle of the night.
- When you find lingerie that does not belong to you.
- When you find gifts like jewelry hidden away and he never ends up giving them to you.
- When he comes home smelling like sex.
- When you find condoms in his wallet.
- When you have to ask your partner if he's cheating on you in the first place.

Remember if you can check off a great number of these signs as being exhibited by your SO, there is probably serious reason to be concerned. At the very least it warrants investigating or initiating a frank discussion with your partner about the health and future of your relationship. Having this conversation is always a good idea. If nothing is going on yet, but the potential for infidelity is looming, then being proactive could possibly save your relationship. The most important indicator that your partner is cheating is if his current behavior differs from his past behavior. If he's always been intensely private about his cell phone and computer or never had much of a sex drive, then these are not indicators that he is cheating. It's the changes in his normal behavior that should raise the red flags for you. If your slobby couch potato is suddenly hitting the gym six days a week and dressing like he's got a shoot for a GQ cover, or your guy who liked to boff every other night is suddenly celibate, then Houston, we have a problem.

Chapter Four

HOW TO KNOW WHEN THE ACCUSED IS LYING THROUGH HIS TEETH

GO UNDERCOVER TO CATCH HIM IN THE ACT

1. HIRE A PRIVATE INVESTIGATOR

If you can afford it, hire a Private Investigator. The good ones are great and worth the thousands it will cost you. They're not supposed to attach a GPS to a person's vehicle, but they do. They provide you with a minute-by-minute report of every single place your partner goes and how long he stays there. You'll know where he shits. Your PI will testify in court on your behalf if you need any of this info in a divorce trial. I hired a PI who kept a dozen changes of clothes in his car, including an array of service uniforms. He could literally get himself inside anywhere unnoticed.

2. SNOOP THROUGH HIS BELONGINGS

Check his phone for calls and texts sent and received. Check all the unidentified numbers. If you don't find anything, he may be innocent, or he may be tech-savvy.

You may have to wait for a time when he inadvertently leaves his computer open and is still logged in, but if you get that lucky check his laptop for emails and private messages. If he habitually deletes many of his emails, that is not a good sign. Check all his social media sites and search his history. A girlfriend installed a key logger on her husband's laptop and got all the passwords to every site he used. Then she logged into all of them. That's how she found out he was online dating. They say you never really know a person and after twenty years of marriage, she had been completely unaware that, according to his online dating profile, he was ten years younger than the age stated on his legal documents (news to his mother), he a had a PhD in Physics (news to her and strange that he had chosen sales over science in his career), had recently spent two years sailing around the world and had no children (news to their two sons). My friend had also been blissfully ignorant of her husband's love for threesomes. With men. When you start snooping you need to be sure that you want to hear the answers to your questions because chances are, they won't be pretty.

Rifle through his drawers, closet, suit jackets, pants pockets, suitcases, wallet, and desk. If he's got a workshop, or spends a lot of time puttering in the garage, I'd check there first.

Read over his bank and credit card statements with a fine-tooth comb. Are there charges at restaurants and bars that don't pertain to business? Check the dates on the charges. Were they made when he said he was elsewhere, or doing something other than he told you he was? I found a number of expensive dinners charged on nights when my husband had told me he was working late at the office, alone.

3. DO A STAKEOUT AND FOLLOW HIM YOURSELF

Do I have to mention the fact that you should not use your own vehicle?

Sit outside his office and watch and wait. Does he leave when he says he's leaving? Does he go where he says he's going? Follow him, but not too closely. It is best to do this with a good friend because it can be a long, boring wait sometimes and because it can get a little nerve-wracking sometimes and because you probably borrowed her car for the stakeout anyway. Also, you should bring a friend especially because it can be really fun and even exciting sometimes! You may have to follow him on foot at certain points, so bring a hat and sunglasses to go incognito. You can also surprise him with a drop-in at his workplace, the bar he said he'd be at with his buddies, the gym, or his mom's home. Just make sure you're prepared to see things that could unpleasantly rock your world, which is another good reason to have a friend at your side.

THE LIE DETECTOR TEST

HOW TO KNOW WHEN HIS PANTS ARE ON FIRE

Don't underestimate your ability to recognize a lie. As humans, we're actually naturally good at it. Our instincts for ferreting out a fibber are quite strong. It's our minds and emotions that get in our way and obscure our judgment. We don't want to believe that someone is lying to our face, particularly if that someone is our Significant Other whom we have loved and placed our trust in. Police, FBI, courtroom experts, and other professionals have turned the process of catching a liar in the act into a science.

As good as humans are at detecting lies, we actually suck at telling them. According to studies, only 4% of us are actually good at lying. We give ourselves up in a hundred tiny ways. With training, you can learn to read these clear signs of deception.

The most important thing is to first determine a baseline, which is the way the individual normally acts. If a person always blinks excessively, talks incessantly, stutters, or usually avoids eye contact, then these cannot be considered signs that they are lying. It's the deviation from their normal behavior, body language, and speech patterns that indicate when a person is lying. Once again, we're looking for CHANGES in behavior.

Who better to understand a person's normal demeanor than their partner? That's right, you are the expert on your SO and therefore you are in the best position to know when he's being deceitful. You just need a crash course in how to recognize the dead giveaways of a liar. It's not that difficult to do and most people can learn the skill in under an hour. However, research has shown that the vast majority of us, up to 99% in fact, do not recognize when we are being lied to. So, it's time to bone up and become bilingual in body language.

Determine how your partner normally acts in regular situations. This is his baseline against which you will measure the ways he acts and speaks when he's being dishonest. If he's normally a laid-back and relaxed guy who's suddenly looking anxious, or if he's usually high-strung and hyper and is exhibiting an uncharacteristic, eerie calm then you need to pay attention. Chances are he's not being truthful.

IT'S CALLED BODY "LANGUAGE" BECAUSE IT SPEAKS VOLUMES:

BECOME FLUENT IN READING IT

When we're under stress our bodies go into "Fight or Flight" mode. It's not something we can control, or downplay. Physical signs are immediately apparent as our bodies automatically react to the stress of the situation and rat us out. Lying is stressful for all but the cream of the sociopathic crop.

TOP 17 BODY LANGUAGE SIGNS THAT HE'S A BIG FAT LIAR

1. His throat becomes dry so he needs to continuously clear it and it can become difficult to speak. The throat's moisture is sent to the skin because the body is sweating as a result of nervousness. He may also bite his lips and require frequent drinks of water.

2. He continuously swallows hard. Lie detecting experts call this the Adams Apple Jump. Moisture, having left the throat area, causes the hard swallowing.

3. He slides his jaw back and forth, with his mouth open. Again, this is the body's attempt to stimulate saliva production to moisten the throat area.

4. His eyes repeatedly shift to the nearest exit, or to his watch. Our eyes indicate the direction that our body wants to go in. A liar wants to get the hell out of Dodge as quickly as he can.

5. His feet point toward the nearest exit. Like the eyes, the feet show us where they want to head. A liar wants to escape the anxiety of the circumstances.

6. His body is quite still. A liar's mind has to work hard to keep his stories straight so waving his arms about, pointing his fingers, or other big gestures are difficult for him. A liar's body may look rigid, almost frozen in place. This is when our bodies prepare for "fight" rather than "flight," readying for conflict. During the course of a normal conversation, people move their bodies around in natural, relaxed, unconscious ways. Lying does not put us in a relaxed state.

7. His head moves back slightly. Liars are uncomfortable because they're afraid of getting caught. He wants to put some distance between himself and the thing that's making him uncomfortable. When we are enjoying someone's company and interested in what they are saying we lean in to get closer to them.

8. His body moves back. Same as the head lean, he's trying to create distance between himself and the source of his anxiety.

9. He covers the base of his throat with his hands. When humans feel threatened, they automatically move to protect the most vulnerable parts of their body like the throat, head, abdomen, and chest. The base of the neck is one of these areas because if something harms you there it obstructs your breathing. If he wears a necklace, he may fidget with it.

10. He makes sudden head movements when you ask him a question. He tilts it to the side, jerks it backward, or looks down.

11. His breathing changes. When you're lying your body is extremely nervous and tense. Your heart rate increases, which alters your blood flow causing breathing to become more difficult. We begin to breathe more heavily. This causes our shoulders to rise and our voice changes, sounding out of breath.

12. He covers his mouth with his hands. Liars don't want to answer the questions being asked. When a liar touches his lips it's because he doesn't want to reveal the truth and is attempting to shut down the communication.

13. He shuffles his feet. A liar is extremely anxious to leave the space. For many experts, the feet are the first things they observe in the person they are questioning. The body tells its story plainly and loudly.

14. He stares too much and blinks too little. Most liars avoid eye contact out of fear of people seeing through them. But some more manipulative liars attempt to take control of the situation by instead gazing intensely at the person questioning them for abnormally long periods, during which they blink less than normal. Some liars blink rapidly.

15. His arm and hand movements become aggressive. If his defensiveness turns to anger and graduates to hostility, he could begin excessively pointing directly at the person questioning him.

16. His true emotions are revealed in Micro Expressions. These expressions only flash across the face for a fraction of a second, but they are visible if you're alert to them. The face will tell the truth before the voice tells the lie. If a liar states that he is not upset about something, he will first display a brief expression of anger on his face. Any feeling of joy, jealousy, fear, contempt, anger, will involuntarily reveal itself on the face for a moment. Most observers can't see Micro Expressions, but you can learn to spot them. (The first season of the TV series "Lie To Me" delves into Micro Expressions and is quite enlightening.)

17. He fidgets unnecessarily. A liar is often restless and anxious, making it very difficult for them to sit still. They may repeatedly perform an action like tidying their papers, clicking their pen, wiping off the table in front of them, tugging at their clothing, or rubbing a spot on their shoes, which action is clearly unnecessary for them to do.

BUILD UP YOUR BUILT-IN BULLSHIT DETECTOR:

THE WAY HE SAYS THINGS REVEALS AS MUCH AS WHAT HE SAYS

Some of us trust everyone, some trust no one. Some of us believe we've got a built-in BS detector that never fails. But all of us at one point, or another are certain that the person speaking to us is lying through his teeth. We're usually not sure how we know, we just do. Our gut tells us this wanker is full of baloney. It's not so much the words the liar is saying, but the emotions he is expressing. What we are actually picking up on is the fact that this person is expressing emotions that are not truthful.

TOP 7 VERBAL SIGNS THAT HE'S PERJURING HIMSELF

1. What he says is inconsistent. He either contradicts himself in his stories, or he contradicts the logic of what a normal person would do in a similar situation. Things don't make sense.

2. His words contradict his physical actions. A person is usually lying when they say something that doesn't fit with their facial expressions, or with the gestures they are making with their body. For example, sometimes a person will say they didn't do something, but unknowingly nod their head yes. Or they may state that they did do something, while slightly shaking their head no. Insincere emotions are not too tough to detect, for example, it's difficult to fake a smile when you're not genuinely feeling happy. The mouth will be small and tight and the lips will be held in the position for too long.

3. He gives too much information and provides too many details. Liars talk a lot in their attempts to convince the people around them that they're telling the truth. They share information that wasn't even requested in their desperate attempts to be believed. When their answers are filled with superfluous details it can mean they have carefully crafted, or even rehearsed their answers. If they are asked what time they arrived home and they launch into a diatribe about the heavy traffic they were stuck in and how they stopped to get gas and the pump was broken and the credit card machine was down, etc., that is not a normal response to a simple question. Too much detail equals lying.

4. He repeats himself. Liars repeat portions of their story and even sentences and words over and over again. They do this partly because they're trying to convince you by driving their story into your head and partly because they are buying themselves time while they concoct the next chapter of their tale.

5. He doesn't use the words "Me" or "I" very often in his speech. Liars do this in an attempt to distance themselves from the lies they're telling. They often use the third person when they speak about themselves, "This is a man who would never cheat on his wife." Or they drop the pronoun completely, "Too busy with work and home life to find the time to have an affair."

6. He states over and over again what an Honest Abe he is. Most liars think that if they say something often enough people will begin to believe it. The most important thing for a liar's success is to project that he is a person of credibility, integrity, and honesty. Therefore, liars will repeatedly make statements like "I would never lie to you" and "I swear on the bible/my mother/my life/our kids/the dog, that I am telling the truth." They start their stories with, "To be perfectly honest…" When people are telling the truth, they don't usually feel the need to go to such great lengths to convince people that they're being honest.

7. He has an explanation for absolutely everything. For most people, it's not easy to remember what they ate for lunch 2 days ago. They have to stop and think to recall details that seemed insignificant at the time, so they didn't make a point of retaining them. When a liar gives an answer he rarely hesitates and he confidently shares his elaborate explanation embellished with verbose details.

I have to admit that my ex exhibits virtually every single one of these behaviors, through both his body language and speech every time we are in court. (And we have been in court over 100 times so far! I know, uuuggghhh. But that is the topic for another book!) When I think back to the days of our marriage and, the times I asked a few too many questions for Dick's comfort, he also displayed the same mannerisms. Unfortunately, I wasn't equipped with this knowledge at that time, so his lies went undetected by me. All I had at my disposal was my intuition and although that was a powerful force that I should have utilized, I failed to take advantage of it. At my peril, I ignored the tiny voice inside me, despite it screaming to be heard. I paid the dear price of time lost on a dead relationship that no amount of intervention could have revived.

Chapter Five

HOW TO PROTECT YOUR RELATIONSHIP FROM A BREAK AND ENTER

IS YOUR RELATIONSHIP AT RISK OF A HOME INVASION?

Sometimes we are truly blindsided by an affair because as far as we knew everything in our relationship was great. The sex was good and frequent and we were happily in love. Sometimes a person can really be that good at disguising their true feelings of discontent. More often things weren't so great, but we're blindsided anyway because we willfully and irrationally chose to ignore the blazing neon signs broadcasting the fact that our relationship was in peril until it was too late to prevent the inevitable shit show that ensued.

CHAPTER FIVE

14 DANGER SIGNS THAT YOUR RELATIONSHIP MAY BE DOA

1. You no longer have fun together.
2. You're leading separate lives and spend little free time together. You may be moving in different social circles, even taking separate vacations.
3. You, or your partner, are risk-takers who crave excitement. The inevitable comfy familiarity that every couple settles into in time can feel like a death sentence to these types.
4. When you are together, even if that's often, you feel like your partner doesn't care about you as much, or treat you the way he used to.
5. You feel distant, disconnected, lonely, or unloved. You rarely have intimate, heart-to-heart talks.
6. You argue. A lot.
7. You never argue anymore because you can't be bothered to.
8. Your friends or work colleagues think affairs are acceptable.
9. You grew up in an environment where you were exposed to affairs.
10. You keep secrets from each other and begin to share secrets with a third party. Once those dynamics are in play boundaries blur more easily.
11. You don't have sex as much as you used to. The sex you do have is lackluster, or unfulfilling.
12. Your relationship is chronically stressed and feels generally unhappy most of the time.
13. You prefer to avoid conflict. Rather than express your feelings in order to have your needs met, you suppress feelings of anger, or resentment and stay silent to keep the peace.
14. You no longer share your joint dreams for the future, or reminisce about the happy times in your history together.

6 WAYS TO BULLETPROOF YOUR RELATIONSHIP

1. Always keep the lines of communication open and use them frequently. Every couple needs those long, intimate talks that occasionally stretch into the wee hours of the night. When the doors of communication close, other doors like the sexual ones close too. **TALK.**

2. Make your relationship a priority in your life. Everybody is busy and tired, but you have to create "Us" time. Don't take each other, or your relationship for granted. Plan regular date nights, share long, slow, weekend morning coffees, afternoon naps and relaxing, evening pots of tea together. Go to bed at the same time to talk, or just read quietly next to each other. Don't underestimate the power of falling asleep in your partner's arms at night. **SHARE.**

3. Keep your loving bond strong. Share your dreams and hopes for the future. Enjoy the excitement of planning the paths you will follow together to reach your mutual goals. **DREAM.**

4. Have fun together. Schedule leisure activities and make playdates. **PLAY.**

5. Make time for love and romance. Put in effort, time and use your imagination. Make each other feel adored, desired, and cherished. It's not difficult, or overly time-consuming. You do remember that your partner loves chocolate-covered almonds, or star gazing, or the smell of burning incense, or a nice chardonnay. Surprise your partner with the simple, thoughtful treats that you know will put a smile on their face. Be affectionate. **KISS.**

6. Make sex a priority. Make sure it's good for both of you. Make time for it often. Make sure your partner knows how much they turn you on. **MAKE LOVE.**

In reality, it's not completely true that a relationship can ever be fully "bulletproofed." The risk of infidelity always exists to some degree for every couple. We can do our best and hope for the best, but we can't control anyone other than ourselves. Affairs aren't accidents or mistakes. They don't just happen of their own accord. People don't inadvertently "fall into bed" with a lover. People who have affairs made conscious decisions that got them all the way to the edge of that bed before they "fell" into it. If your partner tells you that they didn't mean for the affair to happen, then the point is they didn't mean for it not to happen either. Cheating occurs because people make choices and take actions and we always know exactly what we're doing and what the consequences entail. When we embark on a secretive relationship with someone other than our partner, we are aware that we are putting our relationship at risk and harming people we love. Love is the strongest force in the world, but even so, it can't always withstand the abuse some humans willingly inflict upon it. **BE MINDFUL.**

DOES THE EVIDENCE SUPPORT THE CASE FOR THE UPSIDE OF AFFAIRS?

Can an affair be good for a relationship? To be clear we're not talking about couples that have chosen polygamy and are open and honest with each other regarding having multiple partners. We're talking about secret affairs that have broken the trust bond that a couple mutually agreed to. There are those, experts and regular folk as well, who believe that affairs can be a positive catalyst for growth and understanding in a relationship.

I throw the idea out there for anyone for whom it might resonate, but I don't subscribe to this theory personally. I've seen a lot of affairs and I've never known of a relationship that benefitted from betrayal. I know couples that chose to stay together in the aftermath of an affair, usually because of the children, the family business, intertwined or lacking finances, or due to their religious beliefs. In my experience either the cheatee swallowed a ton of personal pride and spent the rest of their years trying not to choke on it, or the cheater was forever punished in that painful purgatory that a trustless relationship breeds. Those couples existed in a living hell of their own creation and I can't say that any of these destructive situations ever seemed like they were "best for the children." Of course, there are exceptions to every rule.

Those who subscribe to the philosophy that affairs can be a positive thing for a relationship commonly believe that:

1. A relationship can recover from and be improved by an affair.
2. It's unrealistic to think that one person can be our everything, every day, for the whole of our lives. Monogamy is not natural, or at the very least, not applicable in our modern world.
3. We're not escaping from our partners when we have an affair we're escaping from ourselves, which can lead to a journey of self-discovery that can help us to understand the deeper meaning of our lives.
4. Affairs can open the communication lines between partners when they share what they discovered about themselves during the course of the affair.
5. The couple can reach a new level of understanding and closeness as they work together to rebuild the trust in their relationship.
6. Affairs can happen to good people who love their partners.

There you have it, the upside of affairs. Excuse me while I leave the

CHAPTER FIVE

room for a moment to puke. But then that's just me. We all get to choose our own paths. More power to you if you're travelling down the reconciliation route. Good luck.

Conclusion

Here's the thing. In all but the rarest of cases, I don't believe that relationships can ever fully, healthfully recover from affairs, but I know for a fact that individuals can. Those of us who have been cheated on and survived to tell the tale are living proof that after enough time has passed, healing will occur eventually. And we can always survive an affair. Broken hearts don't actually kill people they just feel like they might.

Those of us who have been cheated on know for certain that:

1. Affairs can be a positive catalyst that leads us to a deeper understanding of who we are, who we are meant to be and what we are capable of.
2. Affairs can make us better and stronger.
3. Complete trust can never be rebuilt with the scumbag who cheated on us.
4. We don't need that cheater anymore and we deserve better.
5. We can definitely learn to trust again, but we reserve that gift for our worthy, future partners.
6. We can love again, more than ever.
7. We can be loved again, more than ever.
8. If we want it, one great guy, whom I'll call Mr. Right, can be our everything, every day, for the whole of our lives. Potential is

CONCLUSION

limitless.

So the Suspect, who became the Accused, who became the Convicted, is now serving a Life Sentence in a prison of his own making, far, far away from you. You, on the other hand, have been released from a loveless jail and are now free to sail off into the sunset toward the happily ever after of your choosing. You have the world at your feet, strength, and courage at your side, and your dreams at your crown. Peace, love, and joy await and you deserve all that and more goodness in your life.

Remember:

Trust yourself. You alone have the power to make yourself happy and you are a master at creating the life of your dreams. You are a magician. You are a goddess. You are deserving of all good things. The time for transformation, the time to leap off the sinking ship of your old life and dive into the warm, gentle waters of your new world, is now. You've got this.

TALK TO ME, I'M LISTENING

Acknowledgements

To my readers, thank you so much for honoring me with the energy you invested in my book and for placing your faith in me. My aim was to serve you authentically, as well as to entertain, and I hope in some small way I succeeded.

I am deeply grateful to all the booksellers, librarians, bloggers, my enthusiastic Instagram and Facebook community of friends, followers, and bookstagrammers, for championing my work, for reading, reviewing, recommending, and sharing by posting photos, reels, and news, you made a huge difference.

Many thanks to my talented and tireless editors and publishers at Level Best Books, Verena Rose, and Shawn Reilly Simmons, and to the extraordinary SM guru, Kaitlyn Wosik at Social City Consulting.

To all my amazing gal pals and especially to my BFF Dee, I could never have run Life's obstacle course without you.

To my fabulous family— bio, chosen, and spirit, thank you for loving me so profoundly and supporting me so completely.

To Coulton, Roegan, Holden, and Arielle, my astoundingly perfect children, thank you for making my life so achingly beautiful. I am the luckiest woman in the world.

(N.B. To the few horribly toxic people who were in my life, thank you for the hard lessons, I really did learn from you. You were an important part of my evolution but I am grateful those painful chapters are now closed forever. Our ties are cut.)

About the Author

Gabrielle St. George (*aka* The Ex-Whisperer) is a Canadian screenwriter and story-editor with credits on over 100 produced television shows, both in the USA and Canada. Her feature film scripts have been optioned in Hollywood. She is a member of the Writer's Guild of Canada, Crime Writers of Canada, Sisters in Crime, Mystery Writers of America, and International Thriller Writers. Ms. St. George writes humorous mysteries and domestic noir about subjects of which she is an expert—mostly failed relationships, hence her debut soft-boiled series, *The Ex-Whisperer Files*, which launches with **How to Murder A Marriage**. She is also the author of the non-fiction GAL GUIDE SERIES: *How to Say So Long to Mr. Wrong, How to Know if He's Having an Affair*, and *How to Survive the Love You Hate to Love*.

Gabrielle lives a wildly magical life on a fairy-tale farm along the Saugeen River and spends weekends at her 1930s cabin on the shores of Lake Huron with her partner (current coupling still alive and kicking) and their extremely disobedient dogs. When she's not writing, painting, gardening, stargazing, moondancing, and daydreaming, she travels the world to visit her four fabulous children who live abroad.

SOCIAL MEDIA HANDLES:
Instagram: @gabrielle.st.george
Facebook: @gabriellestgeorgeauthor
Twitter: @GStGeorgeWriter

AUTHOR WEBSITE: www.gabriellestgeorge.com

Also by Gabrielle St. George

HOW TO MURDER A MARRIAGE: The Ex-Whisperer Files Book #1

THE GAL GUIDE TO BREAKING UP WITHOUT BREAKING DOWN: How to Say So Long to Mister Wrong

THE GAL GUIDE TO NAVIGATING NARCISSISM: How to Survive the Love You Hate to Love